Popular Performer

2000s

Arranged by MARY K. SALLEE

The Best Songs from Movies and Radio of the 2000s

The 2000s had an array of enduring movie themes and uplifting melodies. This collection revisits these superb hits, casting them in the rich voice of the piano. Music from major motion pictures is represented: "Believe" (from *The Polar Express*, 2004), the main title theme from *Corpse Bride* (2005), "Hedwig's Theme" (from the *Harry Potter* film series, 2001–2010), "In Dreams" (from *The Lord of the Rings: The Fellowship of the Ring*, 2001), and the main title theme from *The Notebook* (2004). The decade was also rich with inspiring songs, such as Michael Bublé's "Everything" and "Home," Jim Brickman's "The Gift," and Josh Groban's "You Raise Me Up." Even veteran rockers Green Day weighed in with their unforgettable "Wake Me Up When September Ends." Revisiting this memorable music is certain to provide hours of enjoyment for the pianist who wishes to be a *Popular Performer*.

CONTENTS

Produced by
Alfred Music Publishing Co., Inc.
P.O. Box 10003
Van Nuys, CA 91410-0003
alfred.com

D1126947

Printed in USA.

ISBN-10: 0-7390-7069-X
ISBN-13: 978-0-7390-7069-7

BELIEVE
(FROM *THE POLAR EXPRESS*)

Words and Music by Alan Silvestri and Glen Ballard
Arr. Mary K. Sallee

Corpse Bride (Main Title)

Music by Danny Elfman
Arr. Mary K. Sallee

Rhapsodic, as if improvising (♩. = ca. 69)

In Dreams
(FROM *The Lord of the Rings: The Fellowship of the Ring*)

Words and Music by Fran Walsh and Howard Shore
Arr. Mary K. Sallee

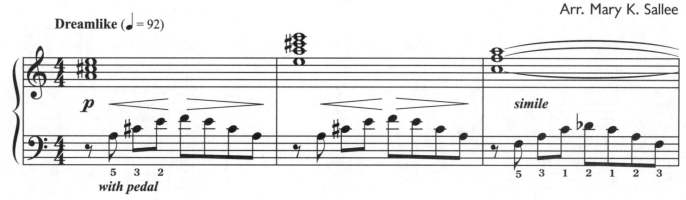

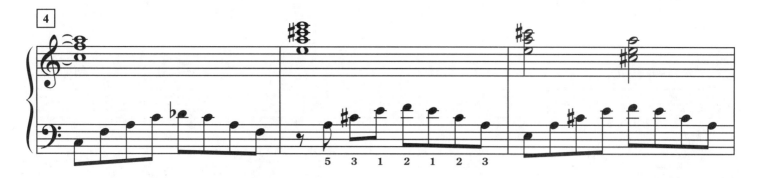

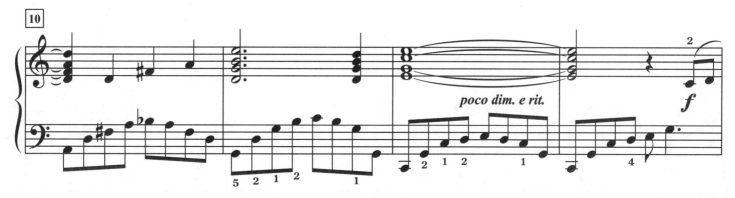

Everything

Words and Music by
Michael Bublé, Alan Chang and Amy Foster
Arr. Mary K. Sallee

THE GIFT

Words and Music by Jim Brickman and Tom Douglas
Arr. Mary K. Sallee

Hedwig's Theme
(FROM *Harry Potter and the Sorcerer's Stone*)

By JOHN WILLIAMS
Arr. Mary K. Sallee

Home

Words and Music by
Michael Bublé, Alan Chang and Amy Foster
Arr. Mary K. Sallee

Wake Me Up When September Ends

Words by Billie Joe
Music by Green Day
Arr. Mary K. Sallee

Smooth and flowing (♩ = 108)

with pedal

bring out lower voice

You Raise Me Up

Words and Music by Rolf Lovland and Brendan Graham
Arr. Mary K. Sallee

THE NOTEBOOK (MAIN TITLE)

Written by Aaron Zigman
Arr. Mary K. Sallee